OPIUM POPPY GARDEN

The Way of a Chinese Grower

BY WILLIAM GRIFFITH

RONIN PUBLISHING, INC

BERKELEY, CA

www.roninpub.com

OPIUM POPPY GARDEN

ISBN: 978-0-914171-67-6
Copyright: 1993 by William Griffith

Project Editor: Sebastian Orfali
Editors: Dan Joy, Ginger Ashworth, Lisa Ruffin
Page Composition: Judy July and Richard Greer
Typography: Genertic Type
Cover Design: Norman Mayell
Photos: William Griffith
Vignettes: Alexander King, from the limited 1939 Ediiton of
Claude Farrer's *Black Opium*, And/Or Press.

Published by
RONIN PUBLISHING, INC.
Post Office Box 3436
Oakland CA 94609

Printed in the United States of America
Distributed to the trade by Perseus/PGW

The Master said:

To know the seeds, that is divine indeed. In his association with those above him, the superior man does not flatter. In his association with those beneath him, he is not arrogant, for he knows the seeds. The seeds are the first imperceptible beginning of movement, the first trace of good fortune (or misfortune) that shows itself. The superior man perceives the seeds and immediately takes action, he does not wait even a whole day. In the Changes it is said: Firm as a r ock. Not a whole day. Perseverance brings good fortune.

—From *The I Ching*
Richard Wilhelm Translation

Opium latex emerging from young capsule at start of
milking process.

Table Of Contents

Opium poppy blossom

Preface

As modern man emerges into the 21st century, the dichotomy between what he knows about himself as a biological organism and what he thinks he knows, becomes the subject of intense scrutiny. On one hand, man knows that there are certain chemical structures to the various foods and other substances ingested into his system. Yet, often these pure substances do not contain sufficient nutrients and when ingested, are not adequate foods. An example of this is the debate over refined sugar vs. naturally occurring fruit sweeteners. While the refined sugar may be the basis of the naturally occurring products in sugar cane, the refined product often leads to disease in the human body. It now appears that the process of digesting the naturally occurring complex carbohydrates in some way allows the body to absorb the sugars without the resulting negative effects of long-term usage. Refined sugar may, in fact, be thought of as a medicine to be used when the body is weak, as it is easily absorbed. As a food to be used in a regular diet,

however, sugar should be excluded and naturally occurring complex carbohydrates used instead.

By analogy, many of the naturally occurring plant
products can be viewed the same way. A tea or infusion
of a pharmacologically active plant may be quite useful
on a regular basis for a wide variety of minor medical
problems, but the refined pharmacologically active product should be limited to short-term medical use. A century ago, it was not uncommon for families to have a
few poppies growing in the garden around their house.
The opium from these colorful flowers was regularly
harvested for use in home remedies, and their pres-
ence in the garden considered to be as natural and
benign as the vegetables that grew beside them. But for
most people today, the word *opium* connotes a link with
heroin. Likewise, the word *coca* today implies cocaine.
This was not true fifty to one hundred years ago. Since
that time, these drugs have been made illegal. The
black market which resulted has required that the physical volume of these illicit drugs be reduced to the bare
essence, resulting in the development of refined heroin
or cocaine as a commercial industry.

The pharmacological activity of a single pure
substance is entirely different from the dilute mixture
of chemically related alkaloids that occur naturally in
plants. In most cases, the properties of these pure substances are so different from the raw plant material,

that they must be administered in a more direct manner, i.e., directly into the blood as opposed to being inhaled or eaten. This direct entry of pure compounds into the bloodstream can lead to negative effects; pure substances are more toxic and an overdose is likelier. When raw opium is smoked, it requires a much longer period of time to get the same morphine content in the blood than it does when administering the morphine directly. This allows certain body defenses, such as sleep or drowsiness, to act, giving the body additional time to distribute the drug in a more dilute form throughout the system. A high concentration of a pure substance can cause shock to the system and be fatal.

In addition to the dilution factor, there is the difference in the chemistry of the raw substance. The effects of the precursors and related compounds may be grossly different from the isolated substance. The non-morphine alkaloids present in opium can have a nauseating effect, so great as to prevent a person from being able to inhale a toxic dose, thus limiting the ability of the user to become seriously addicted. In the psychological reward scheme, a drug with short duration and high reward, such as morphine or heroin, produces the most serious psychological dependency. Of course, in the case of the opiates, physical dependency can create a further problem and risk. If the raw opium is the opiate source, there is much less likelihood of physical dependency.

The economics of distributing these substances has therefore created a much more dangerous situation than existed one hundred years ago. It is more difficult today to find raw opium or coca leaves, and much easier to find morphine, heroin and cocaine. The resultant law enforcement problems have been created by virtue of the illegality, not only of the pure substances, but also of the more dilute, raw product, which has been removed from the marketplace or the pharmacy. In other words, a legal taxed form of the raw product would possibly change the entire framework of the illicit drug market, reducing the cash flow and the resulting crime required to support the economics of this market as it exists today.

Often, drug agencies measure the seriousness of a substance by the monthly deaths incurred. Availability of raw material over refined substances (which have had questionable cutting substances added), would automatically reduce toxic overdoses in the population of drug users. The enforcement of illegal drug laws could then concentrate on monitoring licensed drug manufacturers and preventing the illegal distribution of pure substances.

Raw substances, such as coca leaf, opium and cannabis, might offer preferable alternatives to the substances currently condoned, i.e., coffee, tobacco, alcohol, and various prescription drugs such as Valium. In general, these condoned substances are a part of the work and play model in modern society. Coffee, for instance, is a stimulant often employed by working people, while alcohol is often used after work to relax. The same can be said for coca leaf and opium, which in the raw form are no more addictive than coffee and alcohol. In some cases, the coca leaf may be preferable to coffee because of the negative side effects coffee inflicts on the stomach and heart of some people. Likewise, opium and cannabis might be preferable to alcohol, which is the mostly widely abused drug in our society.

Used in the raw form, some botanicals have a wide home remedy usage beyond the capacity of the refined product. For instance, a tincture of opium can be used as a topical anesthetic on gums of infants cutting teeth. It is also effective in stopping diarrhea in children by slowing the digestive tract. Paregoric (an alcohol tincture of morphine) was available as an over-the-counter pharmaceutical until the middle 1950's. Children raised during the late 1940's and early 1950's generally remember paregoric with positive feelings and fondness for the distinctive flavor without any negative connotations.

But in modern times, the usefulness of raw substances has been largely ignored. Instead, the discount drugstore, with its overwhelming variety of manufactured brands, is the only medicinal source available to us. It is questionable whether these modern products, whose complex ingredients are comprised primarily of refined substances, some of which are impossible to identify and often not as efficacious as the old-time extracts, are the only acceptable resource for our medical needs. It is in this subtext that this book and its discussion of the opium poppy is offered to the reader.

Western society tends to associate opium poppy cultivation historically with China, though in fact the opium poppy was introduced into China by the British. First written references to its use as an internal medicine appear with Hypocrites around 400 BC. Later, it was introduced into India by the Arabians. From India, it was brought to China by the British. During the last 100 years, opium cultivation and use in China has achieved a colorful history, and was also associated with the Chinese in the founding days of modern California. It is because of this cultural heritage, with which we are most familiar, that the setting for the story is with a Chinese family who has emigrated to the New World. The secrets of traditional opium cultivation are expressed in the form of a diary from an earlier generation who grew opium in China at the turn of the century. In this context, perhaps the story of how opium is produced can be accepted, rather than as a story of its production by organized crime for use as the basis of heroin. The separation of the cultivation of a medicinal plant from the criminal element is a positive goal which many Western cultures are moving toward as they struggle with the problems created by the criminalization of natural substances.

Ch'ien's Tale

It was late in the morning when Ch'ien got off the bus in Cahuita. Earlier, while eating his breakfast of fresh fruits in the market square, he'd realized that he wanted his last day in Costa Rica to be a quiet one. He'd decided he would go to a remote area along the beach near Cahuita, just south of his home in the city of Puerto Limon.

Ch'ien walked in the heat of midday. It was sweltering and humid, as only the Caribbean can be. At last he came to a grove of coconut trees. Perfect. He would watch the afternoon drift by from the lofty heights of a coconut palm. Slowly and diligently, he climbed the palm, resting only when he reached the top layer where the coconuts grew. There, he sat down comfortably, like a bird in a nest. No breeze stirred the afternoon, making the heat even more intense.

He performed a few deep breathing exercises. Then, having calmed himself, he brought his consciousness back and gazed out over the ocean. This would be his last look at the Caribbean for quite some time. Though Colombia lay only a few hundred miles south of where he sat, he knew that the best route for him was along the Pacific; for this was the route to the southern part of Colombia, where he planned to seek his fortune. It was a bit more difficult to reach Colombia via the Pacific, but he had heard from other travelers that the northern area of Colombia was already overrun with fortune hunters.

Ch'ien was eighteen now; he wanted to leave home and yet he still had longings to remain with his family. He was certain that what he wanted to accomplish would one day help all of them. How, he wasn't sure, but he knew that leaving Puerto Limon would increase the likelihood of his success. He had grown tired of the life he'd been living there with his family. At eighteen his strength and self-confidence were at a maximum; now was the time for adventure in his life. He'd saved a few pennies from working on the docks. Tomorrow he would begin his journey westward, across Costa Rica.

His thoughts were interrupted by the monotonous creaking of an ox-cart. Along the path behind the grove of coconuts, several ox-carts, loaded down with beautiful hardwoods logs from the nearby forest, rolled by. Mahoganies and exotic tropical hardwoods were always taken out of the forests by ox-cart; these were the only vehicles capable of removing the lumber from the dense vegetation. The result was that all the wood from this area was cut in lengths equal to that of an ox-cart. Because of the limit in length, many of the buildings in Costa Rica were constructed with specially designed beams, made by notching two of these shorter, but beautifully multicolored, hardwood beams together.

Slowly the ox-carts passed and with them, the groaning of the big wooden wheels. Ch'ien was left alone with the sound of the tranquil Caribbean lapping against the Costa Rican shore. He watched as, off in the hazy distance, big freighters carried their cargos of fruit out of, and petroleum into, the Port of Limon. In the steamy jungles on this side of the mountain range, bananas were raised by the millions. There were also large plantations of the cacao plant, whose beans were processed and used to make chocolate. These were the major sources of income for the area .

Ch'ien was glad to have grown up in this region; it had given him contact with people from all over the world, and yet afforded him a very simple and humble life, one which allowed for training of the mind and spirit. Ch'ien had also acquired an expertise in several languages. The area of Puerto Limon was densely populated with Jamaicans, who had come to Costa Rica in the 1800's to build the railroads and work the plantations. From them, Ch'ien had learned English. In fact, one could say that the major language spoken in Puerto Limon was English; a dialect of English, perhaps, but English, nonetheless. It had a certain rhythm that only Caribbean English has. Ch'ien also spoke Spanish, because this was the official language of Costa Rica. He was sure that speaking these other languages would help him in his travels, but at home, with his family, Ch'ien spoke Chinese.

As his thoughts wandered, the hours wore into afternoon. Though the sun was beginning its descent in the west, it was hard to tell that dusk was arriving, since the Caribbean coast was often overcast and cloudy. Living on the coast as he did, he had learned to become familiar with boats of all sizes and shapes. On occasion, he had helped people by working as crew on the various private and small commercial boats that came through. Ch'ien had no fear of the sea and he knew his travels, though long and taxing, would be a challenge for which he was prepared.

Ch'ien surveyed the vastness of the ocean one more time from his perch in the palm. Then, with a contented sigh, he climbed down. He was ready now to return home and spend the evening with his family; the last evening, perhaps, for many years.

He entered the small village of Cahuita just as the bus was about to close its doors and head up the coast to Puerto Limon. Ch'ien broke into full speed and barely managed to catch the door before the driver started off. It was dark by the time they reached Puerto Limon. Gazing through the window at the lights of the ships in the harbor shimmering on the water below, he thought of his adventure and smiled.

Ch'ien listened at the door of his busy household before walking in. His mother and father, brothers and sisters, aunts and uncles were all there, preparing for Ch'ien's last meal at home. They all lived together in a primitive, thatch-roofed house, built on stilts to keep them dry during the rainy season. In modified Chinese fashion, grass-thatched room separators divided the house into small areas for the many inhabitants.

Ch'ien's father had come home early from work to say goodbye to his son. As he looked at his father, Ch'ien's thoughts drifted to his grandfather. He had only known his grandfather for the first twelve years of his life; he remembered him lovingly as an old man with a long white beard and Chinese ways, always wearing a pointed grass hat on his head. His grandfather was always out in the backyard, gardening and growing food for the family table. In fact, his grandfather produced so much food that he had been able to sell his extra produce through Kim Su, Ch'ien's father, at the market. Ch'ien had spent many hours with his grandfather in the garden, working with the wise man who knew the ways of the earth, the wind and the water.

During his childhood, Ch'ien learned all he could from his grandfather about plants, not realizing how valuable this knowledge would be later in his life. It was only after his grandfather passed away that Ch'ien realized the old man had been teaching him much more than how to garden—he had taught him the secrets of *the way.* As Grandfather explained it, once one learns *the way*, practical knowledge will fall into place merely by applying this wisdom. He said that *the way* is an attitude, an openness to understanding, to experiencing, to seeing with the senses what life is and how to aid in this process. He said that man creates nothing; his highest place in the order of being is to facilitate nature by imitating it.

Ch'ien's thoughts returned to his father as Kim Su greeted him warmly and announced that dinner was ready. Sitting at the table with all of his family, as he had done so many times before, Ch'ien particularly enjoyed the wonderfully fresh vegetables cooked by his mother and sister.

After dinner, Kim Su took Ch'ien off to his living area, where they sat in long silence. Though there were no true dividers between the rooms, in Chinese fashion the conversation and thoughts of one room did not travel beyond the paper-thin walls. The other members of the family went about their business and kept to their own thoughts. Each knew in his mind that, in leaving Kim Su and Ch'ien alone, he was acknowledging Ch'ien's parting from the family.

Incense burned in the small room, repelling the evening mosquitoes, though neither Kim Su nor Ch'ien seemed to be overly bothered by them. Kim Su broke the silence. He told Ch'ien that he knew why he was leaving. For this he respected him as a man. His father's father had had to leave his country, too, a century ago, when the family first came to Costa Rica. China had been in a state of turmoil and people were uprooted; some of his family had made it out and some had not. Some had fled to live in parts unknown in areas near Cambodia. The Chinese sense of family, however, was very strong, and there were many relatives in China with whom Kim Su, and his father before him, still communicated. Things had changed considerably over the past one hundred years. Kim Su and his family, though not wealthy by any means, were happy, content and free. It had been Kim Su's father's wish to bring the family together, if possible, and to perhaps one day all live together, as they had many generations ago. Kim Su talked of the earlier generations and how each had carefully passed treasured objects and knowledge to future generations. All of this was contained in the small and ornate box he now gave to Ch'ien. Kim Su explained that he was passing this on to him to do with as he wished. In the box were material objects, spiritual tokens, things of the heart and treasured knowledge from forebears. If, in using any of the materials here, the wealth which was gained could be used to reunite the family, then that would fulfill the wish of Kim Su's father.

Ch'ien sat thoughtfully for several moments. He thanked his father graciously and saved the opening of the box until he was alone. In a most respectful fashion, Ch'ien also thanked his father for all he had been to him and the family. Ch'ien explained that he would be leaving first thing in the morning, before the family arose, in order to catch the early train to the capital city of San Jose.

It was time for Ch'ien to say goodbye to the rest of his family. Everyone was in warm spirits, so the goodbyes were not sorrowful. Once back in his room, Ch'ien turned his attention to the box his father had given him. It contained the *I Ching* (*The Book of Changes*), 64 yarrow stalks, and a silk bag. These were all wrapped in a silk cloth. On the outside of the silk bag were instructions: he was to open it once he reached the shores of the new country. Also in the box, were several small, rather ornate objects of jewelry; each one had been placed there by the previous eldest male in the family as a linear collection of objects through the generations.

Ch'ien removed the objects from the box and placed them carefully in the padded section of his knapsack with his other belongings for the journey. As the instructions indicated, he left the silk bag unopened until such time as he arrived in Colombia

The moon was high in the sky when Ch'ien set his head down on the rice straw bed to sleep and dream his last few dreams while still with his family.

It was early in the morning when he first heard the blast of foghorns from the ships in the harbor. He knew that if he arose now, he could gather his belongings and quietly leave his family, with plenty of time to catch the first train of the day on its way to San Jose. He set out on foot, and in a short time approached the small wooden shed that served as a stopping place for the train. Though he was in the jungle, he was only a few miles outside Puerto Limon; the jungle began where the town ended. The train was the major transportation service for the people in this area, so there were many of these little wooden huts in the jungle over the next few miles. Ch'ien set his belongings down on the wooden platform and waited. Within minutes he heard the sound of the little train, chugging slowly as it pulled its old wooden cars along the tracks, its freight cars heavily loaded with lumber and produce from Puerto Limon. The train stopped and he boarded. This early, the passenger cars were only half full of people, so Ch'ien picked out a good seat by the window which faced forward, placed his belongings on the rack above him, and sat down for the ten-hour journey to San Jose. He'd passed through there only once before, when he was a small child. San Jose was then off-limits to non-white people, so he'd had to view the city from the train window. It was only in recent years that people of color could feel comfortable in the main cities in the central valley of Costa Rica. Ch'ien was looking forward to walking down the streets of his country's capital.

After the conductor collected his ticket fare, Ch'ien leaned back to catch a few extra hours of sleep. The train had to stop in nearly twenty small locations before making the steep climb over the mountains. Ch'ien awoke from his nap just as the train was beginning its ascent. He had been here often enough to be well acquainted with the lush beauty of this transitional area between the coastal jungles and the central plateau. Here, many different fruits and exotic plants were cultivated by wealthy Americans who had come down to start nursery businesses. He once met a botanist who had come here from Florida to set up a wholesale nursery business. Ch'ien had enjoyed spending a few afternoons with this man. The botanist had been open to teaching him many modern gardening techniques because of the natural appreciation for plants Ch'ien had learned from his grandfather.

The train pulled into yet another town on its way to San Jose. Little children came walking up and down the side of the train, selling their edibles to the passengers: oranges, bananas, potato chips, ice cream, soda pop, all sorts of tasty little goodies. Ch'ien bought a bag of fresh-fried potato chips and a bottle of soda pop, leaning out of the window to pay the small boy before the train resumed its climb. As they entered the central plateau, Ch'ien began to see the effects of urbanization. Large homes, obviously belonging to wealthy people, dotted the area. Most of the money had come from commercial coffee enterprises.

At last the train arrived in San Jose. Ch'ien now set out to find his relatives who operated the China Inn Restaurant. His father's directions were excellent; he had no problem finding the restaurant. Once the appropriate greetings were made, Ch'ien sat down to the luxurious dinner his cousins had prepared for him. He had a good night's sleep in the room all to himself that his cousins had provided.

The next morning, he walked across the city to the area where buses left for the Pacific coast. The night before, his cousin had said Ch'ien would find many commercial freighters on the Pacific Coast heading south, but he might really enjoy himself if he could find passage on a small sailing boat. His cousin had met some Americans in the restaurant several days before, who had told him they kept their boat anchored at Playa del Coco, a small beach resort on the west coast of Costa Rica. They'd been anchored there for a week and planned to stay another week before sailing south to Buena Ventura, Colombia. His cousin had said the Americans were vegetarians; they really enjoyed the meal he'd prepared for them. Knowing that Ch'ien and his family were all excellent cooks and gardeners, he had suggested that Ch'ien offer to trade his passage to Colombia in exchange for tending galley.

Ch'ien decided to take his cousin's advice. He boarded the bus for Playa del Coco and, some eight hours later, arrived in the small beach town. Here he was fortunate to meet the Americans almost immediately after leaving the bus. Ch'ien introduced himself and explained the situation as his cousin had suggested. The Americans, Dan and Celeste, were thrilled. They'd just left two other people in Guatemala who'd been traveling with them and were looking for a replacement. Ch'ien more than fit the bill; as a sailor and an excellent cook, he would be a most welcome hand, indeed. The Americans explained that they would set sail in two days. Until that time, Ch'ien was free to do whatever he wished, and he was quite welcome to stay with them on board the boat while awaiting departure. The Americans said they had already stocked the boat for the trip, but because of Ch'ien's knowledge of cooking, they requested he check all their supplies to make sure they were adequate. If anything was needed, they would provide him with funds to purchase the food. They offered to meet him at the dock later on in the afternoon and row him out to their boat in their dinghy.

Ch'ien now had his passage. His mind was at ease as he walked alone along the beach, mentally preparing himself for the long sea voyage to Colombia. The sun was hot and the air was dry, unlike the Caribbean coast. He knew this was something he could get used to very quickly; he merely had to stay out of the direct rays of the sun to be comfortable.

Ch'ien spent the afternoon swimming in the crystal blue waters of the inlet along the quiet beach, until the time came to meet the Americans at their dinghy. As they were rowing out, he read the nameplate on the stern of their boat: "Dedalus" from San Francisco. Ch'ien marvelled at the beauty of the boat. Climbing on board, he felt a deep happiness that he would have the privilege of being on such a beautiful boat traveling to Colombia. Everything on board was neat and tidy. Dan and Celeste obviously loved and cared for it in a manner only seafaring people understand. These people were open and warm, and he knew there would be an exchange of heart. After all the details Ch'ien would need to know for the trip were explained, they settled into a comfortable evening together. An exquisite moon rose over the bay as they shared their first meal aboard the Dedalus.

The two days passed quickly and the few items Ch'ien recommended were purchased. Everyone rose early on the day of departure and watched the sun as it peaked over the hills surrounding the beach, giving the first rays of warmth to the morning. All the necessary equipment for sailing was put in place. Dan figured they could sail right out of the harbor without having to start the engine, as there was usually a breeze at this hour of the day. A device Ch'ien had never seen before was set out behind the transom. Dan told him it was a self-steering mechanism, made in Sweden. It worked by adjusting one fin in the air and another fin in the water; the combination of the two motions created the necessary change on the big rudder to steer the boat automatically. Ch'ien was intrigued with simplicity of this instrument made of nylon and metal. The device merely interacted between wind and water, using the same basic principles of *the way* his grandfather had taught him. In the next few minutes, the sails were hoisted and the journey began. There was a light breeze of 5-8 knots as they set out of the bay, saying goodbye to Costa Rica and land for several weeks.

One day led easily into another. Ch'ien took great pleasure in the company of his traveling companions and the effortless way they went about the routine of sailing the boat. Dan carefully charted their course, keeping constant track of their exact position, while Celeste made sure that everything was running smoothly. Ch'ien found his place. He felt comfortable cooking and was a natural sailor. The weather was good and the wind moderate but constant as they gradually worked their way down the coast to Buena Ventura, Colombia. It was a true seafarer's vacation.

In a little more than two weeks, they reached their destination. They arrived at midday, whereupon they anchored, secured the boat and rowed the dinghy to shore. There, the three travelers shared an afternoon repast of fresh fruit, the likes of which they hadn't seen in weeks. Dan and Celeste decided to spend a few more days in this area of Colombia before heading on to the Galapagos Islands. They needed to get some supplies and send some faxes. Ch'ien read the local newspaper while he waited for them at the American Express office as they sent faxes back to the United States. From what he read about the local news, it seemed as if Buena Ventura had its share of crime. Ch'ien felt the town of Buena Ventura was nothing more than a bad port town. He said his goodbyes to his companions of the past few weeks and wished them well on their journey. Rather than spend the evening with them on the boat, he caught the first bus toward Cali, 175 miles inland toward the center of Colombia.

Cali was located on the other side of the coastal mountain range, in a valley called Valle de Cauca. One of the travelers Ch'ien had met in Puerto Limon had told him about the rare beauty of this valley. He decided he would find a nice spot to camp near there. He'd heard the interior region of Colombia was relatively safe, unlike the jungle areas, and camping would give him the opportunity to collect his thoughts.

At a point midway to the valley, Ch'ien told the bus driver to let him off. By now the sun had set and the intensity of the nearly full moon lit his way as he walked along the road. Soon, he came upon a large meadow where a herd of cows were grazing. He set his belongings down in an area near the far edge of the meadow. At last, he was in Colombia. Gazing at the lovely moon, he found himself wondering about the contents of the silk bag his father had given him. He was rather tired, but he could see well enough in the moonlight to just take a quick peek. He opened the silk bag. Inside of it was a leather pouch and some small, tool-like objects, along with a diary and some written instructions. Ch'ien decided to wait until daylight to properly satisfy his curiosity. He closed the silk bag again and rested his head down to sleep. His mind probed in his dreams, trying to discover the contents of the leather pouch. Gold? Jewels? Silver? He did not know. At long last, he reached the space in his sleep where all dreams stopped; he slept the deep, undisturbed sleep of a man who has just returned to land after a long voyage at sea.

Ch'ien was awakened the next morning by the sound of the cows in the meadow around him. Immediately, his thoughts returned to the contents of the silk bag. He felt somehow it contained an indication of his direction in the next few days. He opened the bag and read the instruction sheet. It told him to open the items in a specific order. First he was to read the diary. This was emphasized by the instructions. The instructions also informed him that there was a piece of land waiting for him in Colombia, in a place called Valle de Cauca. He was to read the diary on the way to this land. Directions were given and he found, to his amazment, that it was not far from where he was now camped. By some instinct, he had actually come within very close proximity to the property. The directions said to go there as soon as possible. Once there, he should begin his spiritual exercises again and, in the family tradition, continue to do the bidding of his ancestors.

With this information, Ch'ien set out on his journey. It took him only two days to arrive in the vicinity of the land designated in the instructions. He found a perch in a tree overlooking the valley, and rested. He had read the entire contents of the diary along the way. He now knew what was before him and what was in the leather pouch. The instructions were clear; the diary described the exact procedures for growing and producing opium from the poppy plant. The leather pouch contained poppy seeds. This was the gift from his ancestors; the result of wisdom gathered over many generations.

That night he camped at the foot of the tree above the valley. He tied the leather pouch around his waist belt before retiring. Putting his hand around it, he slept, dreaming of the land where his future would unfold.

Before Ch'ien's eyes were even open, his nose smelled the faint scent of a cooking fire from a nearby hut. It was about five thirty in the morning and the sun had not yet popped above the horizon. Ch'ien was only the second person in his family to leave Costa Rica and venture out on his own; the first was his sister K'un. He had come prepared for very little, taking only the bare essentials: simple, white muslin pants, a plain cotton shirt, comfortable shoes, a pair of chopsticks, a wooden bowl, a sleeping roll, his copy of the *I Ching*, his yarrow stalks, and the tiny leather pouch which now hung around his belt. Tied to the end of the drawstrings on the pouch was a small ivory carving of a frog and a mushroom. The carving served as a counterweight so the pouch would stay securely around his belt. The artist had cleverly chosen a piece of white ivory that faded to grayish brown for highlights. The delicate frog sat underneath the mushroom, his eyes half-open. Through the underside of the frog and the mushroom were two holes through which the leather strap passed. Ch'ien guarded the pouch carefully, for its contents, together with the information in the diary, ensured his livelihood in this new country.

In those early grey hours of dawn, Ch'ien moved slowly, half in a trance. He sat on his bedroll, facing the east. It was here, in the growing warmth of the rising sun, that he began his daily spiritual exercises each day. This, too, he had learned from his grandfather; to draw inner strength from the reservoir of spiritual energy released by the practice of ancient meditation. While Chi'en's ancestors were Chinese, his family practiced a form of Taoism which integrated Yoga exercises from Northern India with the ancient philosophy of the Tao. He sat with his legs folded in the lotus position, hands extended to his knees, palms up, forefinger and thumb clasped. He relaxed his breathing, closed his eyes, withdrew inward. Having lit an incense stick which burned for thirty minutes, he released himself to the freedom of the inner sounds and let them flow, smiling, drifting, his breathing becoming relaxed, one with the Yogic posture. He had done this many times before and yet, each day it was different. At the end of the burning of the incense, he gradually drew his consciousness back to the plane of the earth. One prostration, and then he began his cleansing exercises. The sun was now appearing above the distant mountains that surrounded the valley. He began with the salute to the sun, his first cleansing exercise of the morning. From this, he went on to his series of stretching, balancing and cleansing exercises, ending with a series of breathing exercises and chanting.

His mind now opened and cleansed, Ch'ien began his morning *I Ching* meditation. After throwing a series of hexagrams with the yarrow stalks, he selected passages from the *I Ching* to read. Ch'ien was accustomed to the sound of the yarrow stalks and to the flow of the motions in gathering them, putting them down and picking them up again. It gave him great peace just to perform the ceremonial actions. Sometimes it was many years before he understood what the hexagrams meant, other times he understood immediately. He did know that they always spoke the truth. This morning, Ch'ien decided to merely throw the hexagrams, record them, and interpret them later. There were some mornings when he went through the ritual of recording them, reading about them to understand their roots, then writing out whole sections of the *I Ching* laboriously by hand and committing them to memory. But today he was anxious to reach his land and begin his career as an opium poppy farmer.

The directions had told him that this land was a present to Ch'ien from his sister, K'un. K'un had married a Colombian named Carlos, and from him she had secured the land for Ch'ien's future. He could build himself a hut and live a simple existence while farming, something he preferred to do while he was young, as his grandfather had done when he was young. It was now December and Ch'ien knew he must begin his farming soon.

By this time, the sun had climbed high in the sky and the heat of the day was intensifying. In the tropics, it seems the closer one gets to the equator, the faster the sun rises and the shorter the dusk and dawn. He hurriedly packed his belongings and set off on the final leg of his journey, wandering along a path that had been made by horse travel. The rugged terrain of this area prohibited travel, except by foot or horseback, and, in these parts, only the rich owned horses. Ch'ien knew that only the simplest lifestyle could adapt to these regions. It was for this reason he was excited about his new venture.

By four o'clock in the afternoon, he had reached his land. It was beautiful; two-thirds of the way up a mountain, level, totally inaccessible, except for one path that led around the side of a cliff, and totally unseen from almost everywhere else. The land was, in fact, more like a shelf hanging on the side of the mountain.

Because of its exposure, it received full sun all day long. There was a stream running down one side of the property. The water was very clean and good. On his trek he had passed a nearby dairy farm. This pleased Ch'ien; he would have manure for his garden and milk for his belly in the months to come. He knew he had all he needed for success.

In the short time before sunset, he checked out his property. Breathing deeply, he felt its expanses and its limitations. The sun set in a spectacular tropical sky of orange and scarlet hues. Ch'ien prepared himself a simple meal of rice and dried seaweed which he brought with him, then lay down to rest on the spot where he'd chosen to build his hut.

The next day, first thing after his exercises and spiritual meditations, he began the cultivation of his land. He set about removing the sod and tilling the soil, hewing and mounding it up in such a way that he could make narrow passageways for the water from the nearby stream. This he did for two more days, until he had the whole one-and-a-half acres mounded and irrigated. The moon was coming on to new moon when he began laying his seed in the ground. The seeds were a special breed, the diary had told him, carefully selected by his forefathers for exceptional strength of purpose; these were the famed opium poppy seeds from China. The particular strain Ch'ien carried was a red variety, more pinkish than crimson, but noted for its exceptionally high yield and high quality opium. He broadcast the tiny black seeds over the moistened soil. The seeds were very fine, so he mixed them with a handful of sand to make the mixture less concentrated. That way, when he sprinkled the mix on the ground, the seeds would be further apart.

This done, Ch'ien now began daily excursions into the surrounding area. At first, he stayed very close to watch the seeds didn't get washed away in any heavy rainstorms. He had saved many of the seeds in his leather pouch in case of such an emergency, but within the first ten days, the seeds germinated and the little seedlings appeared. As the seedlings grew stronger, Ch'ien journeyed farther in search of wild fruit, such as mangos or passion fruit vines. And he travelled down to the nearby dairy quite frequently. In exchange for a few of the smaller gold pieces his family had given him, he was able to get some milk and, of course, he also managed to get some free manure. The manure he valued as much as gold. He placed the manure into a small holding pond he made by diverting some of the water from the stream, and let it stand for a while. Once a week, he would use this pond water to water the fields, as a manure tea. He didn't need to water the plants by irrigation too much. It seemed for one hour every day there was some rain, he was at an elevation where thunderstorms came frequently at this time of year, and then the rest of the day was mild and humid.

One of the benefits of having the dairy close by was the availability of a local fermented milk drink called Kumis, which was absolutely delicious. It tasted like liquid cheesecake with a dash of cinnamon on the top. He had this incredibly luxurious, high protein meal once every other day. The farmer had told him about Kumis. In exchange for this, Ch'ien had given him a few pieces of very special carved jade that had been in his family for many years. He'd regretted doing this, but in the long run, he knew it would make the dairy farmer happy and he would always have a friend, not to mention those wonderful avocados growing in the tree outside the farmer's house.

Within a matter of weeks, the plants had taken hold and their true leaves appeared. His crop was now on its way. From here on it would require more and more attention.

Happy, leading a simple existence, practising his meditation and gardening, Ch'ien made his way into the early months of spring. He was a strict vegetarian and, with the exception of milk, ate no meat products. He had received seeds from the dairy farmer and was growing a wealth of fruits and vegetables in his garden. With the spring thunder showers, Ch'ien began looking for various mushrooms and talking to people who knew about them. He knew his ancestors had gathered many varieties of wild edible mushrooms. He'd heard stories about people from the valley hunting laughing mushrooms, but he did not understand what these were. He promised himself that one day he would get down to the valley and find out what these stories were about. One mushroom he did find occasionally was a common field mushroom. These he relished whenever he found them; he ate them greedily, cooked with a little butter he obtained from the dairy, in a simple earthenware vessel he'd found at the market.

It was April now. The rainy season was over, and each day was warm and sunny, but cooler at night. The plants had taken on their characteristic leafy form and were about to begin their flowering phase. As each one began to sprout a single flower bud, he pinched it off, knowing that pinching one bud would make many more buds form and that, in the case of opium poppies, unlike many other plants, the new flowers would be bigger than the single flower they replaced. Within two weeks, each of the plants had several flower-heads form-ing on them in a circular fashion around the base of the few leaves. As the bud shot up or "bolted," a green-ish pod appeared. Ch'ien watched them, noting that this was the beginning of the flowering phase. After a few days in the warm Colombian sunshine, the pink and red petals inside of these green pods began peek-

ing their way out. By early May, they burst into full
bloom. The flowers only lasted a day or two, revealing a
small seed capsule, the same color green as the rest of
the plant. Inside the tiny vessels within the walls of this
capsule, a white milk would be flowing. This milk was
the purpose of Ch'ien's crop.

In a matter of several weeks after the petals had
fallen off, the capsules swelled; the seeds within these
capsules were ripening. Carefully watching the place
where the petals had previously been attached to the
stem, Ch'ien noted any changes in color and texture, as
well as changes in the color and the top of the capsule,
itself. When he thought these had darkened sufficiently,
he began the process of milking the plants; a laborious
task that would take him two months and require daily
attention. But it was a task he enjoyed, for he knew his
relatives had taught him a secret few other people in
the world knew: the secret of how to milk almost *one
ounce* of the precious raw opium from each plant.

For obtaining the milk, he had a special tool
that had been in the silk bag with his leather pouch. It
was shaped like the sole of a boot and fit into the palm
of his hand. Made of ivory, there were two notches
scored into it on one end. Into the notches he fastened
very sharp blades, barely protruding across the surface
and at an angle so the curvature of the tool would fit
around the capsule. The blades would score the cap-

sule, thereby opening and exposing the milk vessels, but not penetrating through the inner wall of the capsule. By delicately incising each capsule with a series of dashed lines, he could investigate the capsule to see when it was ready for optimum milking. Initially, only a single dashed line was used, so the capsule would not be damaged. As more milk flowed each, the dashed lines were then doubled. Within a few more days, as the flow reached a maximum, he would make a solid double score almost entirely around the circumference of the capsule, early in the morning. On successive days, Ch'ien would scribe it again, but slightly lower than the previous day. In this fashion, he could milk a seed capsule for almost two months. By not penetrating deeply, he would not injure the plant and the plant would remain alive, continuing to function and manufacture more milk. Each day he would go through his entire field, from morning until late at night, scribing all the plants, either with dash lines when they were beginning to flow, or later with solid double lines as the production increased. The next morning, Ch'ien would begin the process of scraping off the dried opium that formed on each capsule. He did this with a spoon that had been ground down on one side so that it just fit around the capsule and he could scrape the opium off. Then he placed the opium in an open leather sack. Once he had scraped the opium into the sack each day, he laid the sack out in the sun to dry. In this fashion, he was able to get many pounds of raw opium from his acre-and-a-half.

And so, the days of harvest turned into weeks for Ch'ien; the only difference from one day to the next was the increase in the size of the ball of opium he was accumulating. He knew it would soon be over. He would miss the intensity and daily rhythm of the hard work.

Several weeks earlier, he had procured a small bag of leaves from a local herbal woman in the neighboring mountains. These were the fabled coca leaves of the Incas, something his ancestors had never experienced. He knew the leaves would be helpful in giving him the energy he needed to continue his long days of toil in the fields. The first time he tried the coca, he placed a small wad of leaves between his cheek and his teeth, along with some baking soda to activate them. He got on the bus to go to town as the pleasant effect of the leaves spread through his body. He noticed that his mouth began to feel slightly numb and there was a warm glow in his stomach as the smooth muscles of his stomach relaxed. Soon, he noticed that several of the Indians on the bus were staring at him and laughing. He realized that, because his mouth was numb, he was drooling the green liquid from the leaves down the side of his mouth and onto his shirt. The Indians knew this was the first time he had tried the coca leaves.

The Indian woman at the market had also given him a small bag of cannabis flowers, explaining that the two together would be very enjoyable, indeed. During the last month of his harvest, he chewed on the coca leaves, occasionally pausing for a few puffs of the very potent cannabis.

Every day he made the rounds to his opium poppies, scribing the plants and scraping the opium from each one; that is, with the exception of a few plants in one corner, which he'd selected to carry the seed for next year. The seed pods on these plants were kept intact and never touched; daily they got bigger and fatter, while the other ones were beginning to show the effect of the continued scarring.

Finally, Ch'ien harvested the last of the opium and finished up the sun drying phase of the production to reduce the water as much as possible. Although he had quite a few pounds of the black gooey substance, he still needed to tend his fields until his seeds ripened, and this would take several weeks. Ch'ien was happy; he was not yet ready to leave the countryside for the city. He still practiced his daily meditations, enjoying the solitude of his home. Like any good farmer, he turned the earth back to restore as much of what he had taken out as he could. He pulled the plants that were finished milking out of the soil and laid them back on top to mulch so their minerals could return to the earth. He knew he must continually enrich his soil so that he could plant again next year. This wisdom his ancestors had given him.

After what seemed an eternity, the seed pods finally dried out and opened up. The seeds were now ripened and ready for the wind, yet, rather than let the wind have them, Ch'ien caught them instead. By waiting a few days and then tapping lightly, he gathered the dark black seeds for next year's crop.

Now he was ready for the final portion of this adventure. He had enlisted a mule from the dairy farmer for transporting his harvest. He left the farmer a small gold coin as a deposit for use of the mule; he would pay the farmer when he returned from marketing his goods and, upon returning the animal, would receive the gold back again. This seemed fair to the farmer, so Ch'ien loaded his summer's work onto the back of the mule and led him to the trail, beginning the journey down into town. He carefully concealed his opium inside empty coconut shells at the bottom of a basketload of coconuts.

During his many months of living in the mountains, he'd had plenty of time to think about what he was going to do with the profits of his labor, and to consider his father's request to reunite the family. Ch'ien wanted to fulfill his father's wishes, but he was young still, and eager to continue his travels. Perhaps he would use the profits from next year's harvest to reunite the family. At any rate, he still had to get his crop to market.

The journey into town took several days. Through his brother-in-law, he was able to meet some people who were interested in his opium. After a very short negotiation, a price was arrived at which was agreeable. Ch'ien unloaded his opium, the result of nearly nine months hard labor. For Ch'ien, it was not the money or the opium, but rather the meditation and the work that was his reward. He had not yet even tasted any of the opium he'd grown. One of the men who'd purchased it, rolled some of the opium into a cigarette of Colombian cannabis and offered it to Ch'ien. This was how Ch'ien preferred it, although he had only smoked opium one time before with some Asian cannabis his father had imported into Costa Rica. Since a room had been provided for him in a nearby hotel, he knew that a long bath and a good night's sleep would be the only two things required of him, so he lit the cigarette and inhaled the sweet smoke, tasting the two essences together.

That night, Ch'ien slept a peaceful and colorful sleep, filled with many pleasant, warm dreams. He slept on a bed with clean sheets, and bathed with hot water, a luxury he'd not known since leaving his parents many months before. In his dreams, he was walking through a field of opium poppies in full bloom, their delicate pink and crimson petals glowing in the morning sun. He awoke happy with the knowledge that he would return again to cultivate his beloved garden. But that was for next year; for now, there was money in his pocket and a world to see.

Excerpt from the Cultivator's Diary

For many generations, our families have made their success farming. Many medicinal plants are known to our family and the opium poppy is one of them. It is part of our tradition to integrate the natural medicines which come from plants into our sense of health and healing. Often, such plants can be poisonous or healing, depending on how these plants are used. A small amount used occasionally can be a medicine. Too much of the same plant may be deadly. By understanding the nature of things, we come to know how best to use the herbs we grow.

Here are the scraps of wisdom we have gathered about the cultivation of the poppy.

Start the plants after the winter solstice if the winter is mild. If there is snow in winter, plant the seeds in the fall after the autumn equinox, so that the plants will start before heavy snow and lie dormant under the snow.

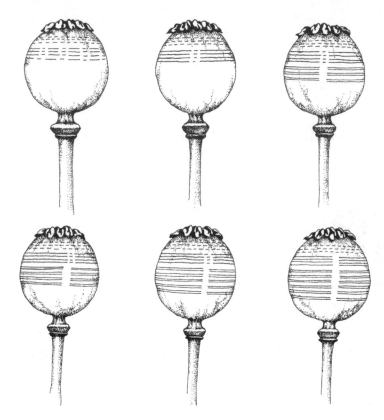

Opium capsule showing successive cuts for
milking using Chi'en's methods.

When the plants are young, give them plenty of
moisture and cow manure fertilizer. After this, they like
fog and mist, but drier soils. As the young plants begin
to send up flower stalks, pinch them back. This may
make many flower buds instead of one bud on each
plant.

The milk of the opium is in vessels in the young
seed capsules as the seeds ripen. This capsule begins

forming the day the flower petals fall from the poppy. The capsule is ready to be milked when the grey band where the petals were attached turns dark—almost black—about 2-3 weeks after flowering.

The milking of the capsule is begun with a tool in which an adjustable blade is used. To make the incision on the capsule, first one blade is used, and later 2 blades are used close together. At the start, only a series of dash-type cuts are made around the capsule near the top. In this fashion, the flow of milk from a capsule can be seen. The depth of the cut is adjusted for the size of the capsule (see photo 7):

Large	1" - 1½"	cut to a maximum of $\frac{1}{16}$"
Medium	¾" - 1"	cut to a maximum of $\frac{1}{32}$"
Small	½" - ¾"	cut to a maximum of $\frac{1}{64}$"

The first cuts are dashes approximately ¼" - ½" long, one per day. A space of about ⅛" is left between first dash-type cuts. The heavier the juice flows, the more the capsule can be cut the next day.

When the flow is full, cuts are made in almost complete circles instead of dashed lines, then with double blades placed $\frac{1}{16}$" - $\frac{1}{32}$" apart. The circle is never completely closed in this cutting or the milk flow stops. Cuts must start at the top of the capsule or the vessels will be broken. Each circular cut is about $\frac{1}{16}$" -

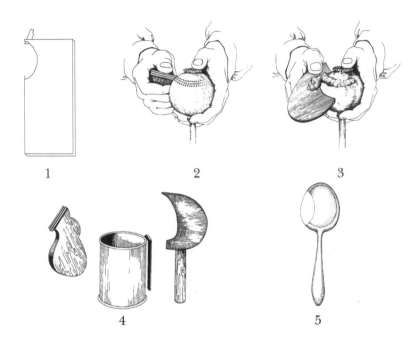

1 - Homemade tool for lancing opium capsule. 2 - Lancing the opium capsule. 3 - Removing opium latex with scraping tool. 4 - Russian tools for opium collecting include lancing tool, cup worn on belt, and scraping tool. 5 - Homemade tool for scraping opium capsule. It is made by filing a spoon.

$1/8$" below the one above. Be sparing in the beginning, milk only a little. The plant will milk for more than a month if the double cuts are started about $1/2$ the way down the capsule.

The milking is begun each morning with the cuts. Later in the afternoon, the raw opium is scraped from the capsule. As the opium is collected, it is dried down as much as possible by drying it in the sun or with artificial heat.

Capsules on several plants must be left completely uncut for good seeds to be produced for the future crops, depending on the number of seeds you need for the next year's crop. When the seeds are ripe, small openings appear at the top of the drying capsule. The seeds that are ripe dry out and become light enough to blow out with the wind. The unripe seeds are still wet and remain below in the chambers of the capsules.

Opium Botanical Description

 The true opium poppy is botanically known as *Papaver somniferum L.* and is a member of the poppy family Papaveraceae. This family contains over 100 species with many varieties. Most of these species are found in central and southern Europe and temperate Asia. Many are well adapted to alpine regions, where water is plentiful in spring and the later summer is dry. All true poppies produce seeds in capsules on long stems, releasing seeds when they are ripe and the capsule has dried out (see photos 2, 3, 4 and 5 of Icelandic poppies and ornamental poppies).

These characteristics are important in classifying poppies. The well known California poppy wildflower, for example, produces no capsule and therefore is actually not a member of the poppy family. Botanically, the California poppy is known as *Escholtzia californica* and is, in fact, a member of the buttercup family (see photo 6).

Of the many species of poppy, only a handful contain the opium alkaloids. *Papaver somniferum* is the

main species used for this. However, there are many
cultural varieties of *P. somniferum*, varying in the color
of flowers and seeds, time until harvest, size of the
capsules, etc. This species is used for the production of
poppy seeds and seed oil for baking (see photo 11).

(Photo 1) Dried opium poppy
capsule after seeds mature.

(Photo 2) Emerging ornamental
poppy flower (non opium).

(Photo 3) Emerging Iceland
Poppy Flower (non opium).

(Photo 4) Ripe Iceland poppy capsule (non opium).

(Photo 5) Dried Iceland poppy capsule (non opium).

(Photo 6) California poppy (non opium, not a true poppy).

(Photo 7) Opium latex emerging from young capsule at start of milking process.

(Photo 8) Young opium poppy beginning flower bud formation. A bud clipped at this stage will produce many more flower buds.

(Photo 9) Opium poppy plant, with emerging flower.

(Photo 10) Mature poppy plant, showing many flowers on one plant.

(Photo 11) Seed bread with seeds from opium poppy.

(Photo 12) Young opium plants, notice leaf shape.

(Photo 13) Emerging opium poppy flower.

(Photo 14) Opium Seed.

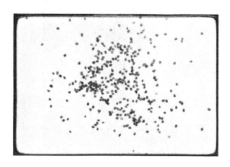

P. somniferum is an annual herbaceous plant, i.e., completing its life cycle in one growing season. The main root is fusiform with some lateral branching into the surface soil. As with other poppies, the plant goes through an initial leafy rosette stage, followed by a bolting to form the flower stalk. The leaves are large, and may be entire, but more often slightly serrated (see photos 8 & 12). The color is green with a blue-grey cast. The plant normally bolts in the spring and produces 3-7 flower stalks (or as many as 15). The bloom and stem appear waxy with grey-green cast. The flower buds are small or all shaped with two large sepals encapsulating the forming flower (see photo 13). These fall off when the flower emerges. The typical opium poppies are the white, violet, pink, or red varieties. Most varieties are single with 4 petals, though some sculptured and double varieties are cultivated. The central single pistil is surrounded by a ring of 150-200 stamens, in 5 concentric circles. The stigma is star shaped with 5-16 rays. Fertilization is usually direct from the surrounding stamens and from 800-2000 seeds are produced. The seeds are usually grey or blue or black (see photo 14).

Ƕorticultural Ƴspects

 Cultivation of *P. somniferum* has certain specific requirements at each stage of development. In order to satisfy these requirements, planting and cultivation differ greatly in different parts of the world. In the beginning or vegetative stages of development, *P. somniferum* requires cool weather and moist soil conditions. Once the flower bud forms and bolts, the plant is readily damaged by water and must be kept dry.

Typically there are two general procedures used in poppy cultivation. In mild regions, where the temperature rarely falls below freezing, the seeds are sown in the spring, in time for the spring rains. For example, in the mountains of Mexico, the seeds are sown in January. In areas of more extreme temperatures, especially areas with snowfall, the seeds are sown in the late fall. The seeds must be sown early enough, however, for the plants to establish a rosette before the snowfall. For example, in Bulgaria, this occurs between September 20th and October 10th.

The seeds can be spread by hand or in rows 2
feet apart. The seeds require a temperature of 37-38° F,
with the optimum at 50-51° F. Young plants like temperatures in the mid 40° F. Severe frosts on open
plantings of young seedlings can be fatal. However,
more developed plants covered with snow can endure
cooler temperatures. Seeds germinate within two weeks.
During the seedling stage, *P. somniferum* requires large
quantities of phosphates. In open agriculture, superphosphate is added prior to seeding. Organic agriculture methods employ turning in bone meal and well
rotted cow manure prior to seeding. Later in the development, more phosphorus, nitrogen and potassium are
added. For example, in commercial cultivation, these
elements are added at the various stages, in the follow-
ing proportions:

Stage	N	P_2O_5	K_2O
Rosette	1.26	.026	1.20
Bud	55.2	18.6	76.4
Milking	61.4	28.3	74.2

(in kilograms per hectare)

In general, phosphorus application is made at
or before seeding, with nitrogenous fertilizer added at
the rosette and budding stage. When possible, manure
is spread and mixed in the soil (15 tons per hectare) in
the season previous to sowing. Then the phosphorus

(superphosphate or bone meal - 30 kilograms per hect-are) is added at seeding time. Once the rosette is estab-lished, a top dressing of manure (or other nitrogen rich source - 45 kilograms per hectare) is made and again at the budding stage, especially prior to irriga-tion.

With the appearance of the flower bud (see pho-tos 8, 9, 10) in the spring, the last fertilization and irrigation (if necessary) are performed. *P. somniferum* requires warm temperatures with no rainfall. A tall stalky plant is easily damaged by rain at this state. Also, the seed-ripening process depends on a warm dry period. More importantly is the effect of rain or moisture on the accumulation of alkaloids in the milky juice.

Generally, the poppy flower lasts only one or two days, after which the flower petals and stamens all drop off and the central pistil remains. Pollination occurs just prior to the flower opening and while it is fully open. After pollination, the central pistil enlarges, form-ing the seed capsule. The capsule is ready for milking 14-16 days or 18-20 days after flowering, depending on the variety selected. The capsule at this time has a blue-grey cast; the abscission zone has darkened where the flower petals were attached (see photos on back cover of this book: Top left **Unripe Capsule**; 2nd down left **Ripe Capsule Ready to Milk**; 3rd down left **Milk Pro-duced by Incising Capsule**).

The milking process involves the laceration of the capsule while the seeds are still unripe. Within the walls of the ripening seed capsule, are vessels containing the opium alkaloids: these vessels are located in the innermost layer of the seed capsule. The outer layer (epicarp) is the skin or epidermal layer; the mesocarp is hexagonal cellular matter and the endocarp has a network of vessels about $1/500$ - $1/800$ inch diameter. These vessels are composed of tubes with sieve plates on the transverse or lateral walls. Poppies of high opium yield naturally have a more developed network of these vessels in the capsule. These tubes are present in the flower stalk and transport the alkaloids from the roots.

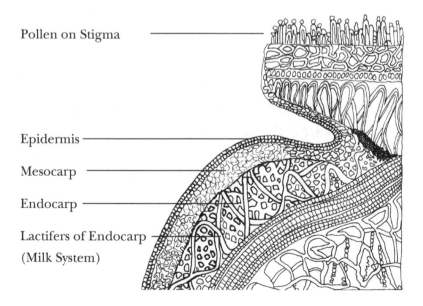

Pollen on Stigma

Epidermis

Mesocarp

Endocarp

Lactifers of Endocarp
(Milk System)

Unlike cannabis, which manufactures its psycho-active ingredients at the local site where it is found on the leaf or flower bract surface, the poppy manufactures its alkaloid pharmacologically active products in the root system and transports this through vessels to the ripening seed capsule.

When the flowering has finished and the seed capsule begins to swell, it is important that the plants be kept under warm and dry conditions. Water in the soil will dilute the milk in the vessels and reduce the alkaloid content.

In addition, the total amount of opium produced is increased under the warm-dry condition. Thus, the plant does its best if flowering occurs during the period of the year with the longest days, i.e., around the summer solstice.

In addition, the largest flow of opium is in the capsule at around midday. It is noteworthy that the alkaloid content is highest when the weather is dry and that more milk is produced at midday on a long day when it's warm; the percent of morphine alkaloid in the opium is highest also at midday conditions. However, the morphine content is highest under shorter day length.

In addition, the morphine content is highest in opium gathered immediately after the vessels have been cut open. This occurs because an oxidation of the mor-

phine alkaloids occurs when exposed to the air. Preven-
tion of this oxidation ensures a higher purity of opium.
The morphine content is highest in poppies sown in
the fall or earliest in the spring (conditions of short day
length). Thus, the seed should be planted in the fall if
the temperature is mild in winter or there is snow to
protect the rosette.

The morphine content of the opium is highest
in the initial 1-3 milkings of the capsule. If one is to
grade the opium properly, only the first and second
milking should be combined. The other alkaloids, such
as codeine, seem to remain constant over repeated milking of the opium poppy.

The raw opium must then be processed in order
to produce drugs which do not contain the other alkaloids. Varieties of opium poppies, such as *Papaver
bracteatum,* have been produced which contain these
alkaloids with no morphine content. Thus the codeine
can be extracted and used for pharmaceutical medicine without the morphine production.

Papaver bracteatum is a native to Iran and was
discovered to contain codeine and morphine. A reverse
example has been discovered in Mexico. Here *P.
somniferum* (n=11) has hybridized with *P. setgerum*
(n=22), a native, non-morphine containing poppy, which
is the common prickly poppy of Mexico. The cross
hybrid contains morphine.

Pharmacology

 The medicinal use of opium predates written history. Images have been preserved from the ancient Sumerians (4000 B.C.) depicting the poppy, along with images indicating euphoria. The first written records of the medicinal use appear from the Greeks, generally attributed to Theophrastus around the third century B.C. The Greeks recognized the euphoria inducing capabilities along with the ability to produce psychological and physical dependency. The term *opium* comes from the Greek word for juice, referring to the latex which forms when the capsule of the plant is cut. Early records indicate that Arabian traders introduced opium to India and China, where the principal use was for the treatment of diarrhea and dysentery. Smoking of opium was not practiced in the Orient until the 1700's. However, by the middle 1500's, opium was used regularly in Europe. Paracelsus (1490-1540) is generally credited with the compounding of *laudanum*. While readily available in Europe, the oral ingestion of opium or laudanum never became the social problem that alcohol became and still is. It was not until the invention of the hypodermic needle by the Scottish physician Dr. Alexander Wood in 1853, that serious problems arose in Western society from opiate addiction. The combination of the syringe and water soluble morphine paved the way for its usage in the American Civil War as a treatment for gunshot wounds as a pain reliever.

Raw opium contains approximately 25 different alkaloids, depending on the variety. The chief alkaloids are:

Morphine $(C_{17}H_{19}O_3N)$ 4-21%

Codeine ($C_{18}H_{21}O_3N$) 0.8-2.5%

Papaverine ($C_{20}H_{21}O_3N$) 0.5-2.5%

Noscapine (formerly called narcotine)
($C_{22}H_{29}O_7N$) 4-8%,

and Thebaine ($C_{19}H_{21}O_3N$) 0.5-2%.

In addition to several other alkaloids (narceine, protopine, laudanine, codamine, cryptopine, lanthopine, meconidine), opium also contains 3-5% meconic acid, either in a free state or combined with other alkaloids. Opium is the only source of meconic acid and tests for this acid are proof of the detection of opium.

Opium historically was used in powdered form (usually 10% morphine) directly or the powder was used to make other remedies. Camphorated opium tincture is also known as Paregoric and used as an antiperistaltic. The dose was 5-10 ml one to four times a day. Laudanum, or tincture of opium, was used in similar applications to Paregoric. The usual dosage of Laudanum was .6 ml four times a day. Dover's Powder or Ipecac and opium powder was made of powdered Ipecac and opium with lactose as a buffer. Dover's Powder was used as a diaphoretic with the opium augmenting the effects of Ipecac by dilating the capillaries of the skin. The usual dose was 300 mg.

Raw opium must be processed in order to produce drugs which do not contain the other alkaloids. Each of the opium alkaloids has a different effect. Thebaine and papaverine have nauseating effects and can make one ill. Morphine is responsible for the dreamy nature of opium and is an anesthetic which is highly addictive. It is classified as a narcotic analgesic; strongly narcotic and hypnotic. The effects are nausea, vomiting, and constipation. A normal dose of morphine sulfate is 10 mg 4-6 times a day. Codeine produces a less dreamy state but effectively blocks pain. Codeine is a narcotic analgesic and antitussive. Its primary medical use is as a sedative, especially as a cough suppressant. It is similar to morphine in action, but less toxic and addictive with less euphoria. A normal dose is about 30 mg 4-6 times a day as an analgesic, and as an antitussive, 5-10 mg, 6-8 times a day. Noscapine (commonly called narcotine) is found in opium as a free base and has no narcotic properties. Noscapine is used medically as an antitussive. The usual dose is 15mg up to 4 times a day. Papaverine is a smooth muscle relaxant. Papaverine comes as white crystals or powder and is odorless, but with a bitter taste. The usual dose orally is 100mg, or intramuscular injection 30mg. Separation of the various alkaloids can be accomplished chemically.

Raw opium is gathered from the incised capsules as the seeds mature within. The exudate is gathered and dried into a gummy mass. Further drying and powdering is required to prepare the opium for chemical separation. The alkaloids of opium account for about 25% of the weight of the dried opium exudate. The alkaloids may be divided into two distinct chemical classes based on the ring structures, *phenanthrene* (morphine, codeine, thebaine) and *benzylisoquinoline* (papaverine, narcotine) derivatives. It can be demonstrated that the phenanthrene group are derived biosynthetically from benzylisoquinoline intermediates, and so the entire group may be considered part of the isoquinoline group (two connected benzene rings with one nitrogen atom taking the place of a carbon atom of the second ring).

Morphine is most readily separated from the other alkaloids. It was the first alkaloid discovered in 1803 by F.W. Sertürner in Germany. This is the first instance in modern plant chemistry in which an active ingredient was extracted from a medicinal plant, and led to the beginning of modern plant chemistry. As a tribute to the Greek god of sleep, Morpheus, Sertürner named the extract morphine.

The structure of morphine was first proposed in 1925 by Gulland and Robinson. Notable are the two hydroxyl groups, one phenolic and one alcoholic, which are of basic importance for the pharmacological effects of morphine. Morphine and its salts occur as white, silky crystals, which can be cubical masses or as a fine powder. It is stable in air, odorless and with a bitter taste. To prepare morphine, raw opium is refluxed in 95% ethanol for six hours. This resultant water alcohol mother liquor is adjusted to a pH of 8.5 with ammonium hydroxide (15% solution). Most of the other alkaloids are insoluble and remain behind. The mor-

phine is then in the solvent and can be evaporated
down to the alkaloid extract. This alcohol morphine
extract (a tincture when adjusted to 3% mixture) is
Paregoric and for many years was available as an over-
the-counter household remedy for diarrhea. Medical
morphine is usually in the form of the sulfate, as this
salt is more water soluble than natural morphine.

Subsequently, Robiquet in 1832 isolated codeine.
Codeine is methylmorphine in which a methyl group is
substituted for the phenolic hydroxyl group. It may be
isolated directly from opium or produced from morphine by methylation. Codeine and its salts are fine
needles or white powder which effloresce in air. Heroin
is diacetylmorphine, in which the phenolic and alcoholic hydroxyl groups are acetylated. Dilaudid
(hydromorphine) is formed by oxidizing the alcoholic
hydroxyl group to a ketone and then the double bond
removed by hydrogenation.

Merck isolated papaverine in 1848. Thebaine dif-
fers from morphine by having both hydroxyl groups
methylated and the ring has been altered by a second
double bond. Thebaine has almost no analgesic effect
and can induce seizures at a fairly low dosage. It is
important, perhaps, in that it can be used commercially
to produce morphine. There is a species of opium poppies (*Papaver bracteatum*) that does not produce morphine, but produces large amounts of thebaine. The

US Government at one point even proposed that this species be used for commercial morphine production, since the raw opium did not contain morphine. The plan was, however, abandoned.

Bibliography

G. Shuljgin, "Cultivation of the Opium Poppy and the Oil Poppy in the Soviet Union." Bulletin on Narcotics XXI (4), October-December 1969: pp. 1-8.

S.N. Asthana, "The Cultivation of the Opium Poppy in India." Bulletin on Narcotics, September-December 1954: pp. 1-10.

D. Daler, L. Slier & R. Slieva, "Poppy Cultivation in Bulgaria and the Production of Opium." Bulletin on Narcotics, January-March 1960: pp. 25-36.

Walter R. Hewmann, "The Manufacture of Alkaloids of Opium." Bulletin on Narcotics, April-June 1957: pp. 34-40.

Louis S. Goodman & Alfred Gilman, *Pharmacological Basis of Therapeutics,* 3rd Edition. Macmillan Co., 1969. Chapter 15. Narcotic Analgesics. Jerome H. Jaffee: pp. 247-249.

Edward P. Claus, Varro E. Tyler, Lynne R. Brady, *Pharmagnosy.* Lea and Febinger, Philadelphia, 1970. Chapter 9: pp. 249-264.

Printed in the USA
CPSIA information can be obtained
at www.ICGtesting.com
JSHW082225140824
68134JS00015B/739

9 780914 171676